I Want A Pickle On My Pancake!

By Jessica Hostetter

ISBN:

Published by:
Holon Publishing & Creative Collective
A collective of authors, artists, businesses, and non-profits.

www.Holon.co

HOLON
PUBLISHING

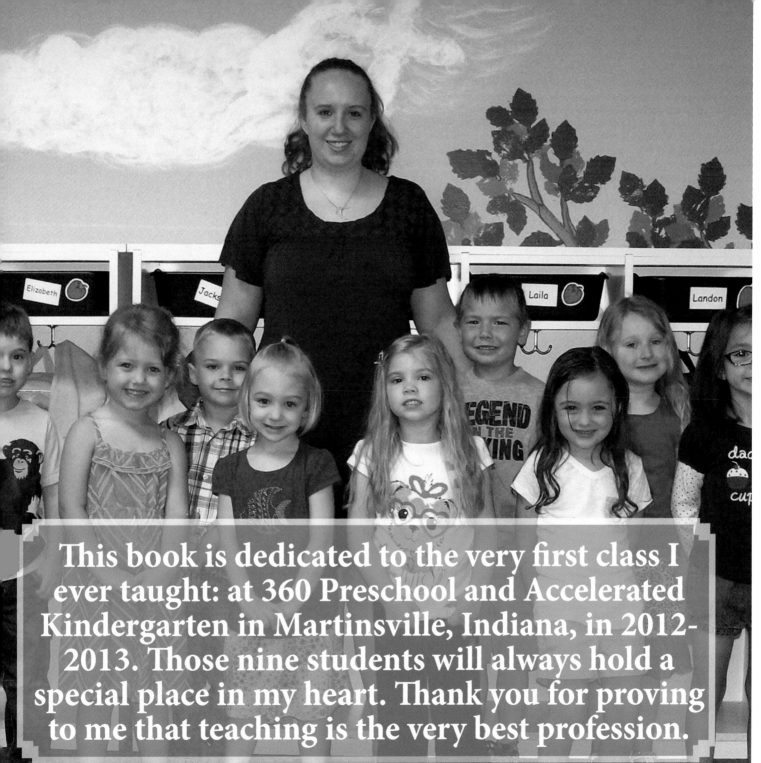

This book is dedicated to the very first class I ever taught: at 360 Preschool and Accelerated Kindergarten in Martinsville, Indiana, in 2012-2013. Those nine students will always hold a special place in my heart. Thank you for proving to me that teaching is the very best profession.

Sometimes, my mom makes pancakes for breakfast.
One day, I asked if I could put a pickle on my pancake.

She said no.

"But why?" I asked.

"Because you wouldn't like it." she said.

"But, I like pancakes, and pickles are my favorite. Together they would be yummy!"

But mom still said NO.

For lunch my mom made chicken soup. "Can I have chocolate cake in my chicken soup?" I asked.

She said no.

"But why?" I asked.
"Because you wouldn't like it!" she said.

"But, I like chicken soup, and chocolate cake is my favorite. Together they would be yummy!"

But mom still said NO.

For dinner, my mom made lasagna.
Can I have lollipops on my lasagna, I asked?

She said no.

"But why?" I asked.

"Because you wouldn't like it!" she said.

"But, I like lasagna, and lollipops are my favorite.
Together they would be yummy!"

But mom still said NO.

I was sad, so I went to bed.

The next morning when I came downstairs for breakfast, I could not believe what I saw!

On the table was all of my favorite foods, pickles on pancakes, chocolate cake in chicken soup, and lollipops on lasagna!

So...

I ATE IT ALL!!!

But, the pickles made the pancakes soggy. And the chocolate cake made the chicken soup taste yucky. And the lollipops in the lasagna hurt my teeth!

Then, I asked my mom if I could have some pancakes, without pickles.

And she said yes.

Cubby's Pickle Pancake Recipe

Ingredients:
- 1 1/2 cups all-purpose flour
- 3 1/2 teaspoons baking powder
- 1 teaspoon salt
- 1 tablespoon white sugar
- 1 1/4 cups milk
- 1 egg
- 3 tablespoons butter, melted
- 1 teaspoon vanilla
- 1 large pickle

In a big bowl, mix together all of the ingredients. Ask an adult to help you lightly oil a griddle or fying pan over medium heat. Pour the batter onto the griddle, using 1/4 cup for each pancake. Brown on both sides and serve hot. Add chocolate chips or blueberries as desired. Before serving, place a large pickle on top. Enjoy!

CPSIA information can be obtained at www.ICGtesting.com
Printed in the USA
LVIW01n1121190417
531341LV00002B/20